Come and See

(Reflections on the life of Jesus among us)

Text by Joy Cowley
Photographs by Terry Coles

Pleroma Christian Supplies

Dedication

To the reader who finds light in unexpected moments. May the blessing of that light reveal to you the beauty of your own dear heart.

Other titles by Joy Cowley and Terry Coles
available from Pleroma Christian Supplies

Aotearoa Psalms
Psalms Down-under
Psalms for the Road

February 2008
ISBN 978-0-473-13191-3
Come and See

Gospel texts from *The New Oxford Annotated Bible*

Design and pre-press: EDiT: www.edit.co.nz
Printed by CHB Print, Waipukurau, New Zealand

Contents

Preface

Joy Cowley has been lovingly taught by God. In 2005 she spent a month with a dozen of us, contemplating the life of Jesus in the Gospels. The venue of that silent retreat (with a day of repose and socialising at the end of each week) at Bellbird Heights, overlooking Lyttleton Harbour, near Christchurch, New Zealand, was enchanting.

I was graced to meet with her for some minutes daily, reviewing how God the Father and Jesus and their Holy Spirit were communing with her, loving her and gently deepening their life in her.

In *Come and See*, Joy and our Lord offer us, not a historical-critical interpretation of the Gospel passages, but something much more enriching. It is all about the now Jesus, the real Jesus, alive and active in the Universe, especially in us.

Joy knows this Jesus and helps us experience Him in people who surprisingly mediate His loving presence for us in unexpected circumstances.

Her book is poetic and beautifully photographed by her husband, Terry Coles. Therefore, it is best read aloud with the photos in view. Let the music of her words soak in to you; repeat the phrases which speak to you. And first be sure to read carefully the scripture passage preceding each reflection. Not to do this is to miss the context and inspiration of her words.

Though nourishing in any place or time, this is specially a bedside book, alone or for couples—one reading aloud and the other listening. Let God's Word become-human soak into you as you prepare for sleep. Let God's love engulf you and bring peaceful closure to your busy, even stressful, day. Yes, come and see! Come and listen!

Feast of the Ascension of our Lord Jesus, May 17, 2007

Fr Armand Nigro, S.J.
Professor Emeritus of Religious Studies
Gonzaga University
Spokane WA USA
Recently at Holy Spirit Center, Anchorage, Alaska

When Jesus turned and saw them following, he said to them, 'What are you looking for?' They said to him, 'Rabbi' (which translated means Teacher), 'where are you staying?' He said to them, 'Come and see.'
John 1: 38-39

1 The Angel Gabriel Visits Mary

Luke 1: 26-35

... the angel Gabriel was sent by God to a town in Galilee called Nazareth, to a virgin engaged to a man whose name was Joseph, of the house of David. The virgin's name was Mary…

GOD WITHIN

Hush, my busy little world.
The voice at the door of my heart
is soft with love
and can only be heard in silence.
"I am Light," it says. "I am Truth.
Let me fill you with my life
and you will give birth to me,
light in the shadows of your house,
truth in the city of illusion."

I know this voice,
better than I know myself,
but still I am greatly afraid.
Lord, I'm so ordinary, so very small.
How can this strange thing be?

I hear the answer before I've asked the question.
"Beloved of God, everyone was made for this.
But it's only the ordinary and the small
who have room for me."

Thought for the Day

The truth of Advent cannot be understood by the usual workings of the mind. The path beyond the mind is through the heart and is called devotion. It is in the heart that we become pregnant with God and give birth to Christ in the world.

2 The Birth of Jesus

Luke 2: 1-7
...she gave birth to her firstborn son and wrapped him in bands of cloth, and laid him in a manger, because there was no place for them in the inn.

HAERE MAI E HEHU

It was getting near Christmas
and just another working day,
traffic nudging time at the red lights,
legs snipping lengths of a busy pavement,
people too separate to be called a crowd,
a day to be registered and counted
in offices all over the city.

But on this day something happened.
Maybe it was the busker with his accordion,
or the laughing girl outside the coffee shop,
or the homeless man on the corner,
bare to the waist and in lotus position,
face and hands lifted to catch the sun,
or maybe it was the pigeons in a mating dance,
feathers shining like oil on water,
or the way a sudden breeze
made the young pohutukawa trees
shiver with ecstasy.

Something disturbed the solemn face of time.
Something shook the folds of perception,
lifting the veil for a golden moment.
In that instant, the busker's music filled the universe,

and people became pure light and lost their boundaries,
and the warm breeze that ruffled leaves and feathers
was recognised as the breath of eternal Love.

Thought for the Day

Our perceptions are shaped by five physical senses: sight, hearing, touch, taste, smell. But we also have five "spiritual" senses linked to the physical. Our senses of beauty, awe, wonder, intuition, love, take us into heart territory where we see beyond usual perception, to the mystery of Jesus' birth in our everyday lives.

3 The Shepherds' Message

Luke 2: 15-20

...Mary treasured all these words and pondered them in her heart. The shepherds returned, glorifying and praising God for all they had heard and seen, as it had been told them.

COME LET US ADORE HIM

Come, all you shepherds and shearers.
Put down your blades,
kick the fleece into a corner
and hurry on down to the birthing place.
Christ is with us.

It is dark right now in Bethlehem
but here the sun blazes in a fanfare of brass
and gulls float like scraps of paper
announcing to a blue, blue sea,
Christ is with us.

Not in a stable this time,
but a house-truck parked down by the creek
under a snow of manuka blossom,
Mary, the baby, two cats and a dog,
and Joseph making pancakes over a little gas stove.
Go quietly now, for this is holy time.
Kick your boots off at the step
and go in with open eyes, ready to be surprised by God.
Christ is with us.

Thought for the Day

If we struggle to understand some details of the historical record of Jesus, we are looking for him in the wrong place. The door to understanding lies in a prayer that brings us to a deep awareness of Jesus born here and now—in us, with us, and all around us. What is this prayer? It is simply love.

4 Presentation in the Temple

Luke 2: 25-26; 36-38
Now there was a man in Jerusalem whose name was Simeon; this man was religious and devout, looking forward to the consolation of Israel, and the Holy Spirit rested on him. It had been revealed to him by the Holy Spirit that he would not see death before he had seen the Lord's Messiah. ...There was also a prophet, Anna the daughter of Phanuel, of the tribe of Asher...

THE TEMPLE

I am Simeon. I am Anna.
For years I have waited in the temple of my life
for the promised Messiah.
Will he come as king, crowned and in purple robes?
Will he be a prophet, Elijah returning in a chariot of fire?
Or a famed teacher and healer, surrounded by young men
who collect every word from his lips?
I tell God, "I see so many people in a day.
How will I find him?"
The inner voice speaks, "You will know,
if you look with the eyes of your heart."

My heart, today, feels the nudge.
I run out, and what do I see?
Two youngsters with dusty feet,
and a baby wrapped in a knitted blanket,
his hand tangled in his mother's hair.
My heart leaps with recognition
but my eyes hesitate.
Can this be the promised Messiah?

God laughs. "What did you expect?
Don't you know that I am always larger
and smaller than your expectations?
This child is the king, the prophet,
the teacher, the healer, the very fire of God,
and he has come, helpless, to live
in the small temple of humanity."

Thought for the Day

Do my expectations of God limit my experience of God, in any way? Does my mind create barriers to my heart?

5 The Boy Jesus in Jerusalem

Luke 2: 41-51

...After three days they found him in the temple, sitting among the teachers, listening to them and asking them questions. And all who heard him were amazed at his understanding, and his answers...

WISDOM

When a wise one speaks to us of truth,
our hearts lean forward, eager to receive.
How delicious truth is to us,
how sweet to the taste buds of the soul!
We feed on it, losing time and place,
forgetting others, even forgetting ourselves,
and we come away feeling nourished
as though from a fine banquet.

Yet this we also know.
The wise one's words of truth
brought to us not discovery but recognition.
All they did was unwrap the deep truth
that had been hidden inside us
from the beginning of our existence.

Truth is the treasure God has chosen
to conceal in our hearts.

Thought for the Day

We are accustomed to evaluating information in our heads, but need also to be aware of what happens at a deeper level. What is true causes something in us to open up like a flower. What is false makes our inner self shut down with indifference.

6 Jesus' Baptism by John

Matthew 3: 13-17
Then Jesus came from Galilee to John at the Jordan, to be baptised by him. John would have prevented him, saying, 'I need to be baptised by you, and do you come to me?'...

DOWN BY THE LAKE

There was a crowd of us down by the lake.
Kowhai petals glowed yellow in the shallows
but the snow on Ruapehu said the water was cold.
Not that it mattered. Just in and out, it was,
with John's voice large over the scene,
and the young folk singing and playing guitars.
Baptism for the forgiveness of sins?
Yeah, right, we thought. A bit of a lark.
But we came out feeling amazing, skin so alive
we could only laugh and gasp and believe
maybe there was something in it, after all.

Then he walked down from the road,
and the music dribbled away to silence.
Heads turned, eyes on him, eyes on John.
Why did Jesus want to be baptised?
Wouldn't it have been more to the point
if he was baptising the rest of us?
But baptism was what h**e** wanted
so John led him over the pumice sand
and into the water, and we watched.
He went in without fuss or flinching,
his gaze fixed on something far away.
His eyes remained wide open
and he went under, lying on his back,

as still as someone newly drowned.
Then just as calmly, up he came,
the water falling off his hair in diamonds,
and suddenly the sun was so bright
that it hurt our eyes to look at him.

Later, I had to ask John, "Why?"
And John said, "Don't you know?
Didn't you feel the change in the air?
He didn't do it for himself.
He did it for the rest of us."

Thought for the Day

Life offers many experiences that are baptismal if we make them so. At night we can give up our day to God before we immerse ourselves in sleep. When we wake in the morning to a fresh day, we can feel God's words passed on to us through Jesus: "This is my Beloved daughter/ son in whom I am well pleased."

7 Temptation in the Desert

Matthew 4: 1-11
Then Jesus was led by the Spirit into the wilderness to be tempted by the devil. He fasted forty days and forty nights...

THE TIME OF TRIAL

Sometimes God calls me into a desert
where I can be alone with my ego.
It is only in some featureless place,
where I can see for miles and miles,
that my vision is clear enough to talk
to that protective, self-centred instinct
which tries to keep me in a prison of one.

When it knows I seek a larger existence,
my ego panics and becomes ugly with fear.
It says, "If you give yourself away,
you'll be physically and emotionally bankrupt."

"Not so," I say. "For it is a law of Life
that what comes back to me
is much greater than what I give."

"But why throw away your success?"
pleads my ego. "You've done well.
You could easily be a big winner."

"The winner is all alone," I say.
"I'd rather be further back,
sharing the journey with others."

My ego is desperate.
"People will not respect you.
They will say that you are mad.

They will laugh behind your back.
You'll be seen as a loser!
Aren't you afraid?"

"Fear is the enemy, little ego,
but the Love that holds us
in its embrace, knows no fear.
Can't you feel its warmth?
Relax, little ego. Go to sleep.
The Lord of the desert is calling."

Thought for the Day

The ego is the voice of our instinct for survival and when it feels threatened, it is loud. Our survival instinct serves us well when we are young, but in maturity we are called to transcend it in order to journey to a larger place.

8 The Call

Matthew 4: 18-22
...And he said to them, 'Follow me, and I will make you fish for people.' Immediately they left their nets and followed him...

FOLLOW ME

At first the call is gentle, no more than a whisper,
a small ripple in the flow of a busy day
and it's only at the third or fourth time
that I stop to listen and then laugh. Who? Me?
This is silly. I must be imagining things.
And anyway, I'm the independent kind,
not made to follow a leader.

The call gets louder and more insistent.
"Leave your boat. Forget your nets.
You are hungering for more than fish.
Follow me, discover the breadth of my life in yours,
and your soul will be filled with the goodness of God."

The call is real enough, but I still don't follow.
To tell the truth I feel rather uncomfortable.
Why should The Holy One seek me out?
I know boats and nets and how to sell fish
and that's all there is to my experience.
Shouldn't he call a better qualified person,
someone who's been trained for discipleship?

But He keeps on saying it. "Follow me."
And when I lift my eyes from my boats, my nets,

and a preoccupation with my separate existence,
I see a world made large by His love.
For the call is made not to me alone
but to every living soul on this planet.
We all have the light of his life in us.
We are all made to feast on the goodness of God.

Thought for the Day

As water takes up the shape of its container, so does God fill who we are. Instead of comparing myself with others, I will try to celebrate the diversity of creation and my unique place in it.

9 Wedding at Cana

John 2: 1-11

...Jesus said to them, 'Fill the jars with water.' And they filled them up to the brim. He said to them, 'Now draw some water out, and take it to the chief steward.'...

THE WEDDING FEAST

The first miracle, the very first,
was not about healing the blind,
or forgiving someone's sin.
The first was the blessing of marriage,
a miracle of wild exaggeration
to match the truth of loving union.
Water turned into vintage wine,
over a hundred gallons of it
for people who'd already
had enough to drink!
Think about that!
What does it say about God
in the midst of our celebrations?
What does it say about life?

Thought for the Day

This is an old Jewish saying: "When a man cannot pray, he should seek God in the arms of his wife." These days we would make the same comment to a woman about her husband. What does this tell us about marriage? And how does it sit alongside Jesus' miracle of water turned into wine?

10 The Beatitudes

Matthew 5: 1-12

...Then he began to speak, and taught them, saying: 'Blessed are the poor in spirit, for theirs is the kingdom of heaven. Blessed are those that mourn, for they will be comforted. Blessed are the meek, for they will inherit the earth...'

THE GIVING OF GOD

He prepares us for this blessing,
in ways we would rather avoid.

Whatever empties us, whatever hollows us,
whatever strips us down to basic existence,
whatever unwraps us, whatever sweeps away
the idols of our own importance,
these things create a space for the truth
of who we really are, and we stand
in the light of new awareness.

When we know who we truly are,
made by God to be filled by God,
then the pain of loss becomes a dream,
meekness comes back to us as strength
and poverty of spirit inherits
riches far beyond naming.

They call it paradox, my friends,
and we need to live it to understand.
It is our smallness that is made
into the greatness of God.

Thought for the Day

An anonymous 15th century monk left these words for us: "Know thyself; 'tis half the path to God, then lose thyself and the rest of the way is trod."

11 Love Your Enemy

Matthew 5: 43-47
'... But I say to you, Love your enemies and pray for those who persecute you, so that you may be children of your Father in heaven...'

THE DIFFICULT COMMANDMENT

Love your enemy. Now, Jesus, that's a hard one.
What about the idiot who rammed our car
in the supermarket park, smashing the bumper,
and leaving not as much as a note of apology;
and the people next door who play
ear-splitting music; and the couple down the road
who don't look after their children?
If people are deliberately offensive,
how can you expect us to love them?

Love your enemy, you say.
That's a commandment, you say.
Well, what do you say about the guy
who spray-painted obscene graffiti
on the wall of our church—your church?
Love your enemy?

All right, I think I've got the message.
When they shoved nails through your hands,
you said, "Father, forgive them,
for they know not what they do."
In the worst of situations,
you blessed your enemies,
and saw them as your friends.

I accept you actually did that.
But you are You. I'm just me.
Where would I get that kind of love?

Okay, Jesus. Don't say it.
I already know the answer.

Thought for the Day

As our relationship with God deepens, so does our capacity for the love that is poured into us in such abundance, that it must overflow into the world.

12 House on a Rock

Matthew 7: 24-29
'...The rain fell, the floods came, and the winds blew and beat on that house, but it did not fall, because it had been founded on rock...'

LESSONS OF EXPERIENCE

It takes some of us a little while to learn
that rock is the best place for building.
My problem was that sand was so easy.
There was so much of it, and it looked stable.
I could put up a house in no time at all
and argue with all the experts
who tut-tutted about the foundations.

I won't bore you with details of the storms
except to say that I felt sorry for myself
and then built another house on the sand.

But in life school, no experience is wasted.
Houses on sand are lessons that shape
our appreciation of good solid rock.
In fact, I think that an apprenticeship
of houses built on sand is more valuable
than the first-time house built on rock,
by someone who didn't know
the sand was there.

Thought for the Day

Let us thank God for error and the courage to own it. Error and failure are two teachers who will eventually bring us the great gifts of compassion and wisdom.

13 Living Water

John 4: 7-14
...Jesus said to her, 'Everyone who drinks of this water will be thirsty again, but those who drink of the water that I will give them will never be thirsty. The water that I will give will become in them a spring of water gushing up to eternal life.'

FLOWING GRACE

In a country of abundant water,
hills and valleys sing with life.
Springs, streams, rivers, lakes,
fill the creases of the land
and flow out to greenness,
making a parable of plenty.

We give three-fold thanks
for the abundance of living water:
gratitude for the greening of the land
in all its variety and beauty;
gratitude for the nourishment given us
in food and drink for life's journey;
and gratitude for the way water speaks
of a larger and deeper life.

For water is the symbol
of an inner abundance
and as we hold out our hearts
for the blessings poured upon us,
we thank the Source of our being.

It's in the fountain of God's love
that we are made eternally new.

Thought for the Day

It is sometimes said that we are all little wells connected to a great underground river. We need to take time each day to fill.

14 The Paralysed Man

Mark 2: 1-5

...Then some people came, bringing to him a paralysed man, carried by four of them. And when they could not bring him to Jesus because of the crowd, they removed the roof above him; and after having dug through it, they let down the mat on which the paralytic lay...

A PRAYER OF GRATITUDE

I thank God for all those people who know
that the roof is no limit for friendship.

How many times have I felt paralysed
by some hard lesson in life school?
How often have I been unable to move
through fear, loss, or a forbidding challenge,
and the world has passed me by?

But then, always, along came friends
who picked me up and carried me,
as though I had no weight at all,
and indeed I did feel lighter
with their loving support.

Through them, I felt the touch
of the Healer, and rose from my mat,
learning something new about growth
through death and resurrection.

Oh, dear God, help me to be
a friend like that!

Thought for the Day

Every painful experience is a birthing event, but for that new life to happen we need to be midwives for each other.

15 Dinner at the House of Levi

Mark 2: 13-17

...As he was walking along, he saw Levi son of Alphaeus sitting at the tax booth, and he said to him, 'Follow me.' And he got up and followed him. And as he sat at dinner in Levi's house, many tax collectors and sinners were also sitting with Jesus and his disciples—for there were many who followed him...

TE WHARE ITI

Jesus, for years I ate and drank at your house
but didn't dare invite you to mine.
Actually, the house of my life
was small and rather shabby,
the furniture well worn,
some of it less than comfortable,
and I'd forgotten to clean the windows,
which meant it had become a bit dark.
"He wouldn't want to come here,"
I told myself. "He's in great demand.
He has important places to visit."

So I didn't invite you, Jesus,
but that didn't matter to you.
You invited yourself, and barged right in,
filling my house with your light.
Before I could apologise for the mess,
you made yourself at home,
so enthusiastic, anyone would think
you'd waited years for this occasion.

To tell the truth, when I looked around
I saw that my house was quite beautiful,
and it seemed it was made for you.

Thought for the Day

With the Lord's light within us, our vision is transformed and we are able to see beauty everywhere.

16 'Come to Me All You That Are Weary'

Matthew 11: 28-30
'Come to me, all you that are weary and are carrying heavy burdens, and I will give you rest. Take my yoke upon you, and learn from me; for I am gentle and humble of heart, and you will find rest for your souls. For my yoke is easy, and my burden light.'

REFRESHMENT

Today, Lord, I do not have a loving heart.
It has grown tired, like a wilting flower
in a drought-stricken garden,
and I am burdened with self-reproach
because I have nothing more to give the world.
It happens, this, from time to time,
and being tough on myself is dry comfort.

Great Lover, I need time to rest beside your oasis,
to fill up with the waters of your sweetness
and be nourished by your eternal kindness.
You will hold me until all my shoulds and should nots
fall away like last year's leaves and I will feel again,
green growth beginning a new season.

Then my heart will remember what my head forgets,
that the greatest gift of your love
is your life in me.

Thought for the Day

Jesus calls us to find rest for our souls.
Can we take time out of this busy day to do just that?

17 Through Him All Things Were Made

John 1: 1-5

...All things came into being through him, and without him not one thing came into being. What has come into being in him was life, and the life was the light of all people...

AOTEAROA JESUS

Lord, that day on the beach,
I saw your footprints on damp sand
between foam and drifts of pipi shells,
and like a child, I placed my feet in them,
my heart leaping with recognition.
"You are here, God! You walk with us!"
You laughed in the sun-soaked air and said,
"Dear One, I've always been here.
Simply look with the eyes of your heart."

After that, I saw you in the bush after rain.
You were a light in every tree and fern,
a bright burning that gathered all creation
into a shining Oneness, and I felt like Moses
standing awe-struck, on holy ground.
"You are here, God! You walk with us!"

You touched the eyes of my heart,
when you danced on Auckland harbour,
when you sang with the voice of a tui
in a tree in parliament grounds.
But it was today that you showed me
your deepest and dearest secret.
You wore a suit, a sari, pink jandals,
a jacket with a gang patch, rosary beads.

You were on a bike. You drove a Honda.
You did a fancy leap off the footpath
on your brand new skateboard.
You had a latte in one hand
and a cellphone in the other.
Dear Lord, you were everywhere!

Then I saw my reflection
in the window of a shop
and my heart stopped in wonder.
You are here, God!
You walk in me!

Thought for the Day

Sometimes the last place we look for God's presence is in our own lives.

18 Be Merciful

Luke 6: 36-38
'Be merciful, just as your Father is merciful. Do not judge, and you will not be judged; do not condemn, and you will not be condemned. Forgive, and you will be forgiven; give, and it will be given to you...'

THE BUCKET

I think it takes a lot of years
and an understanding of how life works,
to be truly wise, truly compassionate;
and somewhere along the way we learn
that life is like an empty bucket.
What we put into it
we take out with interest.
Maybe that's what Jesus meant
when he said to his disciples,
"Give and it shall be given to you."?

What do we put in our buckets?
It's a complex question
that will have a complex answer,
but it is the desire of our hearts
to offer just the one thing
that God gives us in abundance—
LOVE.

Thought for the Day

Sometimes we love the wrong things too much and the right things too little, but the voice of guidance in our hearts helps us to make the right choices in the way we love.

19 The Transfiguration

Matthew 17: 1-8
Six days later, Jesus took with him Peter and James and his brother John and led them up a high mountain, by themselves. And he was transfigured before them, and his face shone like the sun, and his clothes became dazzling white...

AORAKI

Jesus, the mount of transfiguration
was perfect that day, with fresh snow
glittering white under a blue sky.
The earth had reached up to a rare height
and heaven came down to meet it
and you stood, at the pinnacle of life,
looking at a view far beyond
the walls of your incarnation.
You were as young as the moment,
older than forever, and from this place,
Jerusalem must have seemed far away.

Jesus, on Aoraki, your sacred mountain,
you grew beyond our knowledge,
and we were overcome by awe.
How could we speak to you?
Was this the travelling companion
who beat us at cards last night?
The one who burned the morning toast
while giving the rest of the bread to birds?
Now we had to shield our eyes
to look at you, and all our words
were frozen by that light.

You returned to us, changed but not changed.
There was snow in your hair. Your hands were warm.
Laughing, you reached down and showed us
how to make snowballs from this thing called Time.
And then, we understood who you were.

Thought for the Day

Where will I meet God today? Will the meeting depend on the place or my state of awareness?

20 The Lord of the Sabbath

Matthew 12: 1-8

...When the Pharisees saw it, they said to him, 'Look, your disciples are doing what is not lawful to do on the Sabbath.' He said to them...'if you had known what this means, "I desire mercy and not sacrifice", you would not have condemned the guiltless. For the Son of Man is lord of the Sabbath.'

NEIGHBOURHOOD WATCH

Be alert for the outsider, the one who doesn't fit.
Be alert for the one of no fixed abode.
Be alert for the one who challenges authority.
Be alert for the one who treats saints and murderers
as equals in the name of love.
Be alert for the one who has no respect for property.
Be alert for the one who turns your values upside down.
Be alert for the one who disturbs your peace.
Be alert for the one who follows you like a beggar,
demanding your everything.
Be alert for the one who conceals his identity in your heart.
His name is Jesus.

Thought for the Day

We can be sure that in following Jesus we will be emptied before we can be filled with a greater life. It is part of his crucifixion and resurrection gift to us.

21 Sparrows and Lilies

Luke 12: 22-31
'...Consider the lilies, how they grow: they neither toil nor spin; yet I tell you, even Solomon in all his glory was not clothed like one of these...'

LITTLE THINGS

Holy One, we thank you for small things:
the blue butterflies in summer grasses;
the fragile toadstool pushing up
through a crack in the pavement;
the wheeling flock of sparrows
scattered across the sky like tea leaves;
the single note of a bellbird
marking the end of day.

Sometimes, we get so caught up
with our own notions of importance
that we need You to remind us
that You are in the details of our lives,
present in every cell of our being,
present to every action in our day.

Butterflies, plants, birds, grasses,
everything comes from your Oneness,
bearing something of your light,
and everything returns to you,
in your great dance of Creation.

Holy One, when I'm measuring
the world's bigness against my smallness,

and am feeling alone and inadequate,
remind me to look at butterflies
and sparrows and lilies of the field,
and the way You shine
especially bright,
in small things.

Thought for the Day

Someone said that the difference between a flower and a weed is a judgement. When we cease placing judgmental labels on ourselves, and the rest of creation, we see divine beauty in all.

22 Prayer

Matthew 6: 5-6
'... whenever you pray, go into your room and shut the door and pray to your Father who is in secret; and your Father who sees in secret will reward you.'

SACRED SILENCE

As we come near holy ground,
we undress our minds
and lay the garments of thought
at the side of the road.
We do not carry the judgements
that we place on ourselves and others.
We let fall our opinions of evil
and our notions of goodness.
They belong to the mind
but not to our gentle hearts.
Next we take off our religious shoes,
all those ideas about the right way
to worship and the right steps to take
to show our devotion to God.
They are important in their place
but not here in this inner sanctum.

Do we feel naked?
Do we feel vulnerable?

Then it is time to proceed,
bare and simple, to the place
where we will be clothed
in the radiance of Love
far beyond human thought.

Thought for the Day

Half an hour of silent prayer in the morning is like swimming out to catch a current that will carry us all day.

23 The Trinity

John 14: 15-17
'If you love me, you will keep my commandments. And I will ask the Father, and he will give you another advocate, to be with you forever. This is the Spirit of truth, whom the world cannot receive because it neither sees him nor knows him…'

GLORIA

Glorious are you O Mystery of Life,
essence of all creation.
You are the symphony of stars and planets.
You are the music of the atoms within us.
Forest and farm, the rush of the city,
everything is held in your love.

We rejoice as we sing our gratitude.

Glorious are you, O Jesus Christ,
cosmic love in human flesh,
our brother, teacher and friend.
You make your home in our lives,
daily revealing that cross and resurrection
are one on the road to freedom.

We rejoice as we sing our gratitude.

Glorious are you O Spirit of Truth.
You are the needle of the inner compass
always pointing to true North,
guiding us in the dance of love
that takes us to the heart of the Mystery of Life.

We rejoice as we sing our gratitude.

Thought for the Day

For centuries the Church has sung traditional songs of praise to the Holy Trinity. Can we create a personal "gloria" from the gospel of our experience?

24 Flowing Life

John 7: 37-38
'..Let anyone who is thirsty come to me, and let the one who believes in me drink. As the scripture has said, "Out of the believer's heart shall flow rivers of living water."'

THE RIVER

Life is like a river that flows towards the sea.
It has a small beginning, increasing gradually
until it's in a larger place, a current deep and wide,
giving its abundance to the land on either side.

And I have questions to ask you, my friend.
Where does the sea begin? Where does the river end?

The river has its secrets. In its depth it knows
the nature of the ocean where its water flows.
It hears the seabirds singing. It feels the touch of foam.
The sea is always calling the river to come home.

And I have questions to ask you, my friend.
Where does the sea begin? Where does the river end?

Life is like a river and deep inside my mind,
the call of love grows stronger as I leave each day behind.
We're moving with the current of this unseen mystery.
Already we have knowledge of the presence of the sea.

And I have questions to ask you, my friend.
Where does the sea begin? Where does the river end?

Thought for the Day

I believe that in the spiritual dimension, time is not linear. Spiritually we are like rivers, connected to our source and our destination as we travel through the world. The knowledge that the entire journey is held by God runs deep within us.

25 The Parable of the Sower

Mark 4: 2-9
'...Listen! A sower went out to sow. And as he sowed, some seed fell on the path, and the birds came and ate it up. Other seed fell on rocky ground, where it did not have much soil, and it sprang up quickly since it had no depth of soil...'

GROWTH

I thank you, bountiful Sower,
that you do not choose good soil alone.
You cast your abundant blessings
over the entire landscape of existence,
knowing that conditions can change
and barren soil may become fertile ground.

My old hard paths of judgmental thought
have become softened by a rain of tears
and are ready for new growth.

My stony places have small patches
of rich soil that are waiting
to receive the seed of truth.

And last year's crop of thistles
has mouldered down to a compost
that will grow strong plants
and a good crop of fruit.

I am so grateful, bountiful Sower,
that my growth does not depend
on my unstable earthly condition,
but on your endless abundant giving.

Thought for the Day

God uses all of our experience. Sometimes the most barren or weed-choked soil will become the most fertile ground for the loving sower.

26 The Command

Mark 16: 15
And he said to them, 'Go into all the world and proclaim the good news to the whole creation.'

DO YOU MEAN ME, LORD?

Go into the world and preach the Gospel.

Jesus, what's this you're asking?
I'm neither prophet nor teacher.
You know that. Do you expect me
to stand on street corners
telling people the good news?

Go into the world and preach the Gospel.

I get it. It's not so much about words
as living the truth of your teachings,
love of God and love of neighbour,
and letting my actions do the talk.
If you don't mind me saying so, Lord,
that's even harder than the street corner.

Go into the world and preach the Gospel.

I can't even get my own life in order.
How can I live your truth for others?
You call me to an impossible task.
Oh, I see, Lord. It's your life in me
that will be good news to the world.
All I have to do is allow myself
to be filled with your love. Is that it?

Go into the world and preach the Gospel.

If you don't mind, there's one last question.
How do I get so filled with your love
that it overflows into the world?
Stay close, you say. It's as simple as that?
If I stay close to you so that my heart
grows warm and soft with your presence
it will fill with love for all creation?

Okay, Jesus, I'll give it a try.

Thought for the Day

When faith becomes imprisoned in the head, it can raise all manner of irrelevant questions and make Christian life seem difficult. The experience of God's love can be known only by the heart.

27 Casting Nets into Deep Water

Luke 5: 4-11

When he had finished speaking, he said to Simon, 'Put out into deep water and let down your nets for a catch.'...

THE DEPTHS OF PRAYER

Most of the time, I exist on the surface of life,
grateful for the taste of God in everyday experience,
but seldom venturing out beyond the shallows.
In fact, this intertidal busyness becomes so normal
that I forget what deep water can do for the heart.

Then guidance speaks through the clamour—
gentle but insisting until it is heard.
"It is time to push out your boat
into deep water and drop your net."
And my little boat, steered by a hungry heart,
leaves the shore of small concerns and goes out
to the deep, deep waters of silence
to drop a net into the unknown.

I've forgotten how scary it is out here
in the realm of unmeasured stillness.
I look at my watch. My hands feel lost.
My brain scampers like a mouse on a wheel.
But gradually, the net of prayer sinks
into that space beyond actions and words
where it is so filled with light and peace
that I don't want to return to the shore.

Except I know that the shallows and the deep
belong to the same great sea of life
and I need them both for spiritual health.

Thought for the Day

Jesus' public life was balanced by times of solitude and prayer. Are we able to take time away from our busy lives to fill up with the deep peace that recharges our spiritual life?

28 The Centurion's Servant

Luke 7: 1-7
...The centurion sent friends to say to him, 'Lord, do not trouble yourself, for I am not worthy to have you come under my roof...But only speak the word and let my servant be healed.'

A CERTAIN KIND OF FAITH

We all know folk like that centurion,
people with mountain-moving faith,
for whom prayer is as natural and essential
as food and water and sleep.

One such friend has a reputation
for powerful prayer, and a prayer list
that takes an hour or more each day.
When I asked her what the secret was,
she was surprised. "God's love is no secret,"
she said, and then she thought for a moment.
"Well, there is something—a bit like a secret.
Years ago, I made a promise to God
that I'd never pray for myself—only for others.
If I prayed for myself, it wouldn't work."

"But what about your own needs?" I asked.

She smiled. "Oh, God knows what they are
before I even know them myself.
I reckon I can leave my needs to God."

I went away inspired and a little envious.
I wish I had faith like that.

Thought for the Day

On our faith journey we carry words that have been so well used they are almost weightless. One of these words is "prayer". Let's sit with the Lord for a while, thinking about prayer, how we use it and what it means to us.

29 The Daughter of Jairus

Mark 5: 22-24, 35-42
...He took her by the hand and said to her, 'Talitha cum', which means, 'Little girl, get up!' And immediately the girl got up and began to walk about (she was twelve years of age).

LITTLE ONE, ARISE

On the road of life, we meet pain
in different shapes and conditions.
Small deaths will overwhelm us
with loss, loneliness, betrayal,
and our lovely hearts may feel broken.
Sometimes, we lie in a night of sorrow
that seems without hope of sunrise.

Yet it's in this consuming darkness
that we find the seed of pure light.
This is where we hear the voice
that has always been within us.
It says, "Come, little One, arise!"

Wonderfully, the seed of light grows
until it floods us with new strength,
and a new kind of knowing,
and we emerge like butterflies
from a chrysalis of transformation.

"Come, little One, arise!"

This, we discover, is the truth
of crosses and resurrections,
two aspects of the one event.
Every death, be it small or big,

is leading to a larger place,
while he, who went before us
to show us the way of growth,
keeps calling with love,
"Come, little One, arise!"

Thought for the Day

God gives us unfailing light so that we can journey into darkness without fear.

30 The Parable of the Good Samaritan

Luke 10: 29-37
'...Which of these three, do you think, was a neighbour to the man who fell into the hands of the robbers?'

THE SAMARITAN STORY

It was a dangerous part of town at night
but being a stranger, he didn't know that,
and they beat him with a baseball bat,
took his watch, money and credit cards,
and left him, near death, on the pavement.

The mayor, on his way home from a meeting
that had been bad for his blood pressure,
noticed the figure lying on the footpath.
"Drunk," he thought with more than a little envy.
"What I wouldn't give for a whiskey right now!"
And he put his foot down on the accelerator
to shorten the time to his front door.

The couple returning from the dinner party
were taking a detour through back streets
to avoid the breath-testing stations.
When the woman saw the man in the shadows,
she shivered and touched her husband's arm.
"Poor fellow," she said, "asleep on the street.
The government should do something
about these homeless people."

The girl from the nearby escort agency
said goodbye to her client, put on her coat
and stepped into the street, almost falling over
the dark shape lying in a darker pool of blood.
She screamed. "Oh God! He's hurt bad!"

Her hands shook as she jabbed her cellphone.
"Ambulance! No I don't know what happened.
Maybe he got hit by a car. You'd better be quick."

He was groaning a little, so she took off her coat
and put it over him. It was fake fur but warm.
Then she sat on a step near him, rubbing her arms,
telling him everything was going to be all right,
help would be coming any minute.

Paramedics put the injured man on a trolley
and wheeled him to the waiting ambulance.
She climbed in after him, her coat over her arm.
"I'm going to make sure you jokers look after him,"
she said to the paramedic who sat beside her.
"Are you a relative?" he wanted to know.
"Yeah, I'm his grandmother," she said.
"Come on! The guy's in a bad way.
Just get him to the hospital like now."

And somewhere, in another time
and place,
but echoing as clearly as when first
spoken,
someone was asking Jesus, "Master,
tell us who is our neighbour?"

Thought for the Day

When he was asked, "Who is our neighbour?" Jesus talked about a hero who was a despised Samaritan. In this context I ask myself, "Who is my neighbour?"

31 Feeding the Crowd

John 6: 5-13
...Then Jesus took the loaves, and when he had given thanks, he distributed them to those who were seated; so also the fish, as much as they wanted...

LOAVES AND FISHES

This loaves and fishes miracle, it is fact.
It is truth. He does it for each of us
in response to our spiritual hunger.

It starts with the smallness of self,
me, my little lunch, my little faith,
God wrapped up in ideas
and labelled me and mine,
and what happens?
Jesus happens.
He takes the little package,
opens it up, and before we know it
he's made a childhood faith
into a feast fit for thousands.
How does he do that?

The feast is for all who hunger
for goodness, and it is free.
There are no labels, no restrictions.
No one is asked to provide details
of their identity or religion.
Food for the spirit! More than enough!
Loads and loads of love left over
for giving away to others!

Our little faith is made huge,
and it is all miracle, all gift.
The only thing we can offer in return
is gratitude.

Thought for the Day

When Jesus said, "Give and you will receive," he wasn't talking pious nicety. This is the law of God's universe. Whatever we give will come back to us with increase.

32 Calming the Storm

Mark 4: 35-41
...He woke up and rebuked the wind, and said to the sea, 'Peace! Be still!' Then the wind ceased and there was a dead calm. He said to them, 'Why are you afraid? Have you still no faith?'...

ROUGH JOURNEYS

Weather speaks in parables
that neatly fit our experience.
I look for summer sunshine,
blue skies, warm days, calm air,
and I fret about wind and rain.
It's only after many seasons
of voyage on this sea of life
that my judgements shift
and I understand storm and calm
as two aspects of the one event.
It's this whole death-resurrection thing,
a movement through pain to renewal.

It's not that I like storms.
I will always feel vulnerable
when the wind howls in my face
and waves break into my little boat.
But Jesus has done this before
for my sake, and for yours,
and we can rest in the knowledge
that he always sails with us.

Thought for the Day

Given the choice between comfort and pain, what do I choose? Certainly, not pain! Yet there is no growth in comfort. The journey to true freedom lies through storms of pain and grief, with just enough still water to give us time to reflect on what the storm was all about.

33 The Healing of the Blind Beggar

Luke 18: 35-43

... when he came near, he asked him, 'What do you want me to do for you?' He said, 'Lord let me see again.' Jesus said to him, 'Receive your sight; your faith has saved you.'...

LORD, PLEASE LET ME SEE

Maybe he was on Highway One
with his bedroll and backpack,
jerking his thumb at the traffic.
Or she could have been at the checkout
in the supermarket, dreaming
that some beautiful young man
would rush in and rescue her.

Who they were, doesn't matter.
The fact is, we are all on some kind
of road, leaning blind into the future
and praying, Lord, let me see.

The prayer may be held in metaphor,
Lotto, astrology, the wishbone of a chicken,
plans for the wedding of the year,
or promotion, or retirement, anything
that is connected to tomorrow.
Lord, let me see.

Very gently he reminds us
that there is no tomorrow or yesterday,
only the eternal present moment.

If our minds are in the past or the future,
we live like ghosts, blind beyond reach,
for it is only in the here and now
that he waits with his healing touch,
to open our eyes to the light.

Lord, let me see.

Thought for the Day

Simple sensate experience has hardly been respected as a spiritual tool, yet it is our senses that bring us to the present moment where we experience the Sacred.

34 Mary and Martha

Luke 10: 38-42
Now as they went on their way, he entered a certain village, where a woman named Martha welcomed him into her home. She had a sister named Mary, who sat at the Lord's feet and listened to what he was saying...

ACTION AND CONTEMPLATION

She knows them well, these sisters of faith.
They are a part of her daily routine
and mostly, they share her existence.
But this morning the Martha in her is busy,
buttering bread for school lunches,
cooking porridge, making a shopping list,
moving the dog away from the cat's food.
She hasn't yet had a chance to comb her hair,
and the rest of the day will be just as heavy,
so when the Mary in her suggests
that she sit at the feet of the Lord a while,
she says, "Not now! I don't have the time."

But outside the back door, she sees
a perfect yellow rose hanging over the fence.
Its beauty stops her and she says to herself,
"Through him all things were made,"
and the words are all that is needed
to open the door of her heart.
The Mary in her takes her by the hand
and leads her into the stillness
where her Lord is waiting for her.

Again she remembers the truth of service.
Mary and Martha cannot be separated.
One takes in and the other gives out,
in a natural rhythm like breathing.

She doesn't know how long she stays
in the fragrance of his presence,
but afterwards, her heavy day
seems as light as a feather.

Thought for the Day

Moments of prayer in a crowded day bring peace to the heart and an ease to work.

35 Becoming Like Children

Matthew 18: 1-5
...He called a child, whom he put among them, and said, 'Truly I tell you, unless you change and become like children, you will never enter the kingdom of heaven...'

SIMPLICITY

When I was young, a tree was simply a tree,
but as I grew, I learned that the tree
was made up of separate parts
and that each part had a name:
leaf, bud, twig, branch, trunk, root.

Yet I grew some more, and found
the tree could be divided further
into cellular structure and function.
I learned names like xylem and phloem,
cambium layer and photosynthesis,
and in the fascination of discovery
I lost sight of the simple tree.

Still I grew, and with the gift of age
came a return to simple vision.
The parts of tree came together
to form a oneness with the earth,
a oneness with me, and I saw
that we were all gloriously alive
with the light of our Creator.

And you know something?
I think this is the journey

that Jesus was talking about
when he said we must become as children
to enter the kingdom of heaven.

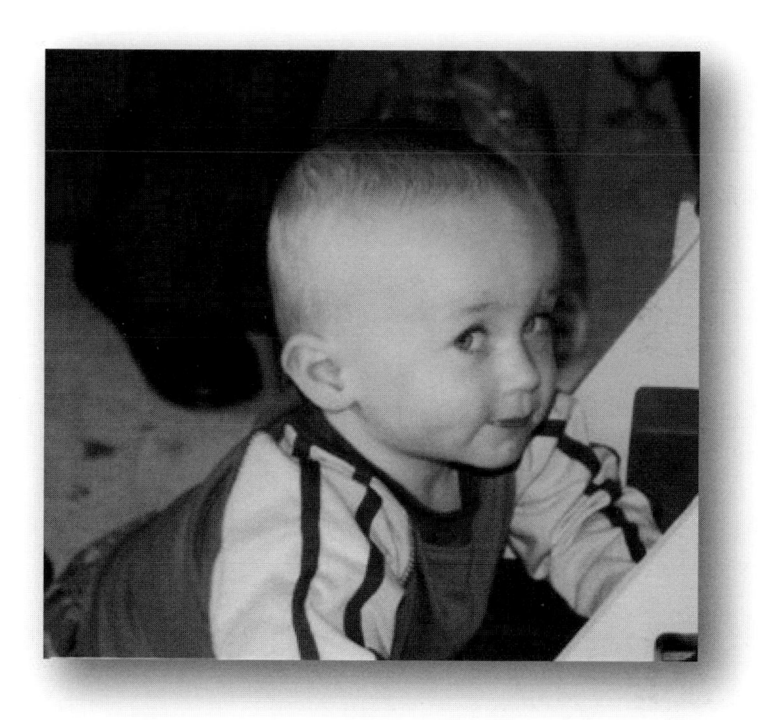

Thought for the Day

Jesus said that we should become as little children to enter the Kingdom of Heaven. He didn't say we should "remain" as little children. The journey back to the beginning is a long one, and I think it's what Jesus meant when he told Nicodemus (John 3) that he must be born again.

36 Zacchaeus the Tax Collector

Luke 19: 1-10

...He was trying to see who Jesus was, but on account of the crowd he could not, because he was short in stature. So he ran ahead and climbed a sycamore tree to see him, because he was going to pass that way...

SONG OF ZACCHAEUS

Always, our darkness contains a seed of light
that struggles to grow into brightness.
Evil so hungers for good that often
it will consume itself in its longing.
For light is the truth of all existence.

Holy One, I have always known
the bright sparks of your presence in me.
You shine like a star in my nights,
creating in me a great longing
to once more be one with you!

But I am small, Lord, one of your anawim,
and I do not see over the crowds.
I'll do anything to attract your attention,
work, pray, climb the tree of yearning
and recklessly crawl out on its branches.

Oh Lord, come to me
so that I may come to you!

When at last you are sitting at my table,
and my entire house is aglow with you,
I ponder on the mystery of my darkness.

Would I have recognised my need for you,
if my life had been as bright as the day?

Thought for the Day

The tensions in this life can cause division in our thinking and sometimes we can try to reject our shadow without examining it for the growing point that will bring us to God's Light.

37 The Parable of the Yeast

Matthew 13: 33
He told them another parable: 'The kingdom of heaven is like yeast that a woman took and mixed in with three measures of flour until all of it was leavened.'

THE LEAVEN IN THE DAY

The thing about yeast is we need so little of it
to put some lightness into a stodgy day.
There's the man at the newspaper stand
who's always ready to throw us the smile
that we carry away. We toss it in the air,
see the way it bounces off other faces.
One smile can lift an entire street.

A laughing child swings around a post,
hair and jacket flying, and we remember
how it feels, how the weight of the body
on a rigid arm propelled us, and suddenly,
instead of that weighty problem at work,
our thoughts are suddenly as light as air,
celebrating the freedom of childhood.
Yeast, yeast, wonderful yeast.

We can find yeast in something as small
as a butterfly or a pumpkin flower,
or the purr of a well-tuned engine,
or the crunch of fresh shortbread,
or the way the light falls across
the feathers of a pukeko in a paddock.

Yeast is everywhere, my friend,
yes, everywhere, little bits waiting
to be scooped up by our senses.
It doesn't take much to fill a heavy world
with the lightness of God.

Thought for the Day

What is yeast to my day? What fills me with gratitude? What makes me alive to the beauty of God around me and in me?

38 The Rich Young Man

Matthew 19: 16-26
...Jesus said to him, 'If you wish to be perfect, go, sell your possessions, and give the money to the poor, and you will have treasure in heaven; then come, follow me.' When the young man heard this word, he went away grieving, for he had many possessions.

CHOOSING

There was once a rich young man,
who knew it all, had it all.
This young man so filled his life
with comfort, material and religious,
that he didn't know
he was living in a padded cell,
didn't know he was actually poor,
until he met Jesus.
Until a crack appeared
in the wall of the cell
and the light shone through.
Ah, but glimpsing the light
is one thing.
Getting rid of all that comfort
to live in the light
is another.

That rich young man is in me.
Will he break out of his prison?
Or will he turn away, sorrowing?

Thought for the Day

When God calls us to step into the unknown, most of us will choose the comfort of what we know. It's as well for us that God keeps on calling.

39 The Pool of Siloam

John 9: 1-7
... he spat on the ground and made mud with the saliva and spread the mud on the man's eyes, saying to him, 'Go, wash in the pool of Siloam'...Then he washed and came back able to see.

THE POOL

Yes, I know it, this pool of Siloam.
It's in the bush at the back of the farm
and I met him there unexpectedly,
mistaking him at first for the sound
of leaves and the rustle of a tui's wing.
I was blind you see, blind as a bat,
having been told that God lived
in some far-off place called Heaven.
To me this was just a patch of bush
smelling damp with a small pool
fed by a spring that bubbled out
of stones, with green fur of moss
like a cushion at the edge.

I'd just stopped to catch my breath.
That was all.

There was no kind of warning.
Perhaps He did come on the wind
that shifted the kawakawa leaves
or on the quick clip of the tui's flight.
All I know is that suddenly,
the eyes of my heart were touched

and I knew that He was there,
behind the surface of everything,
a light that turned trees to fire
and filled all the spaces between.
I knelt in the moss and grasses
at the edge of the spring-fed pool
and washed my face with holy water.
Everything, yes, everything
shone with his presence
and I laughed, drunk with light,
I could see! I could truly see!

Thought for the Day

When we know creation we know the Creator, for He wears this world like a garment.

40 The Blessing of Children

Matthew 19: 13-15
Then little children were being brought to him in order that he might lay his hands on them and pray. The disciples spoke sternly to those who brought them; but Jesus said, 'Let the little children come to me, and do not stop them; for it is to such as these that the kingdom of heaven belongs.'...

BLESS US, LORD

Lord, when you blessed little children,
you also blessed every adult,
for childhood is not in our past
but the pure state we carry with us,
still connected to you our Source.
And so, Lord, we ask you to bless us.
Bless the vision of the lovely heart
that sees the world as fresh and beautiful.
Bless the trust that neither judges nor condemns.
Bless the quick sense of awe and wonder
that opens us up wider than wide.
Bless the lack of fear that makes space for love.
Bless the lightness of foot, rhythm of dance
and music of every present moment.
Bless the laughter that rings in us like birdsong.
Bless our softness of touch and wetness of eye.
Above all, bless our childlike curiosity,
for it is our seeking that brings us full circle
to the joyous freedom of simplicity.
And in that freedom, oh Lord, bless us
with the sweetness of rest in you.

Thought for the Day

Jesus tells us that spiritual fulfillment brings us to a childlike state. I think of the beautiful souls I know who have this gift, and I am grateful for the light they share with the rest of us.

41 The Good Shepherd

John 10: 14-16
'I am the good shepherd. I know my own and my own know me, just as the Father knows me and I know the Father. And I lay down my life for the sheep...'

ON THE ROAD

On the hottest day of the year,
he came down the road with his sheep,
moving them from the hill paddock
to the grass down by the stream
where they could wade through watercress
and lie under the weeping willows.

He took his time because they were slow,
some old ewes amongst them, part lame,
some of them stressed with heat,
a few late lambs uncertain of direction.
His boots were the colour of dust
and his shirt patched with sweat,
but his smile was fresh as morning
as he apologised to waiting traffic,
adding a word or two of thanks.

Sitting in the car, in that hot white light,
we thought of deserts, of history,
of the Good Shepherd who knew his sheep,
and two thousand years of meaning
were suddenly clear to us.

Sometimes we are sheep, stressed, lost,
in need of the Shepherd's tender care,
and sometimes Jesus calls us
to be today's good shepherds.

Thought for the Day

Life is fluid, ever changing. Sometimes we are shepherds; sometimes we are sheep. Jesus knew this. He was the Good Shepherd who became the sacrificial lamb.

42 The Woman with the Haemorrhage

Mark 5: 25-34
...He said to her, 'Daughter, your faith has made you well; go in peace, and be healed of your disease.'

TOUCHING THE UNTOUCHABLE

The law was very clear about this:
she was bleeding; she was unclean.
If she touched a man, he would be defiled.
So for years she had been treated like a leper,
exiled from her marriage bed,
pitied by other women who knew her.

What made her so bold that day?
Desperation? Awareness of the Holy One?
Did she feel her heart drawn towards him
in a certainty that was beyond the law?
Whatever, she came up behind him
and touched the edge of his cloak,
and his energy filled her with healing.

We know it. We've all been there.
At times the law has drawn lines around us
and put up signs that say "No Trespassing"
and "Admission to Members Only".
But the presence of the Holy One
makes us bold and in that moment
we know there is only him and us.

We feel the connection. He feels it.
In the contact, we are bonded by light,
and a burden falls away from us
as though it has never existed.

What will he say to our touch?
Will he judge us as unworthy?

He shrugs at the law, smiles at the signs
and holds his hands out to us.
"Your faith has saved you. Go in peace."

Thought for the Day

The law is not an enemy. It is a valuable teaching tool. The law can guide us towards the place where we connect with God, but it can't be that connection. Healing happens beyond it, in the territory of the heart.

43 The Curse of the Fig Tree

Mark 11: 12-14, 20-21
...Seeing in the distance a fig tree in leaf, he went to see whether perhaps he would find anything on it. When he came to it, he found nothing but leaves, for it was not the season for figs. He said to it, 'May no one ever eat fruit from you again.'...

THE BARREN TREE

I didn't understand that story about the fig tree
until the morning I was waiting for the bus.
There was frost in the gutter, steam in the air,
and a crowd of us with red ears and noses
jiggled and stamped to keep ourselves warm.
Then he came along, the homeless man,
newspapers tucked inside his jacket,
grey hair, grey beard, blackened nails.
Of all the people at that stop, I was the one
he targeted, shuffling sideways, eyes fixed
on mine and fierce with intent. "Hey, lady!
Got spare change for a hungry body's breakfast?"

He wouldn't be ignored and he refused
the small but firm shake of my head.
With everyone watching, he stood in front of me,
hand outstretched. "A couple of bucks'd do it."

I told him in no uncertain terms what I thought.
It wasn't my season for giving. Every week
there was some collector at this bus stop,
holding out a bag for a donation.

I'd already done my share. If he wanted food,
he could go down to the soup kitchen.

He lowered his head and shuffled away,
clutching the newspapers inside his jacket,
and as he wandered along the road,
toward someone else's bus stop,
I felt something inside me wither and die.

Thought for the Day

Jesus wears many disguises. We are least likely to see Him in the poor and the very rich.

44 The Widow's Offering

Mark 12: 41-44
… he called his disciples and said to them, 'Truly I tell you, this poor widow has put in more than all those who are contributing to the treasury. For all of them contributed out of their abundance; but she out of her poverty has put in everything she had, all she had to live on.'

THE OTHER GIFT

All she has to offer are two small copper coins,
not enough to buy a measure of oil.
But they'll have to do. She has nothing else.
She ties them in the corner of her shawl
and hurries to the temple.

All I have to offer are a couple of talents
that struggle like cabbages in a weed-filled garden.
In a world that is desperate with need
they make a pitiful contribution
but I have nothing else to give.
I decide to offer them to him.

When she comes to the temple,
she sees riches poured into the treasury
and her heart falters with shame.
Oh, if only she had that kind of wealth
to offer to her God!

When I come to prayer, I know my poverty.
I think of people like Nelson Mandela
and Mother Teresa, who have done so much,
and I'm almost paralysed by my inadequacy.

She makes her offering apologetically,
hoping that no one will notice,

but as she leaves, she sees him,
the one they call Jesus the Nazarene,
and his gaze surprises her.
"Your offering is beautiful," he says.
She doesn't know what he means
but she understands the love in his eyes.

I tell Jesus that my talents are nothing,
just a couple of old cabbages
from a weed-choked garden.
His reaction is surprising.
"Beautiful!" he says. "A lovely gift!"
Then he adds, "But if you don't mind,
I'd like to have the weeds as well."

Thought for the Day

God's unconditional love is not earned or bought. All we have to do is accept it. It will fill every part of the space in our lives that we make available.

45 The Truth Will Make You Free

John 8: 31-32
Then Jesus said to the Jews who had believed in him, 'If you continue in my word, you are truly my disciples; and you will know the truth, and the truth will set you free.'

FREEDOM

This truth, this freedom, this music of the heart,
we all have it within us, but well wrapped,
layers of paper and knotted string in the way.
Nonetheless, at quiet moments, we feel a stirring
and we hear beyond hearing, some sweet note
that we recognise from another time and place.

What is this truth? What is this freedom?

Truth is not held in words, and yet the unwrapping
comes with words, slowly, one layer at a time,
until truth is finally revealed as a bright light
beyond the horizons created by the mind.

With each unwrapping we exclaim,
"I know it! I know what Jesus meant!"
for this is the thing about truth.
When someone speaks truth-bearing words
we experience the delight of recognition,
as what was hidden within us
comes into the light of freedom.

And once we have that freedom,
no one can take it from us.

Thought for the Day

The heart is wise in all things, so we need not concern our minds with what is true or untrue. What is untrue for us will pass lightly over us and disappear, and what is true will come home surely to our hearts.

46 The Lord's Prayer

Luke 11: 1-4
He was praying in a certain place, and after he had finished, one of his disciples said to him, 'Lord, teach us to pray, as John taught his disciples.'...

EFFECTIVE PRAYER

The way I see it, Lord,
there is outer prayer and inner prayer,
words written for the eyes and mouth,
words spoken for listening ears,
words stumbling along in the mind
falling over each other in an attempt
to express the inexpressible,
words rushing up from feelings
of love or gratitude or distress.

I guess it's all effective prayer, Lord,
when it comes your way
with a little push of the heart.

Yet the prayer that I long for
is not held in words but in silence
when the body is hushed
and the mind is as calm
as a lake on a breathless day.

It is then that we journey, Lord,
far beyond our thoughts, to the place
that we knew before we were born,

a place of truth, dear and familiar,
where your love is like a lamp
in a window, welcoming us home.

Thought for the Day

Sometimes God speaks to the heart in a language that the head does not understand.

47 The Bread of Life

John 6: 27-35
... Jesus said to them, 'I am the bread of life. Whoever comes to me will never be hungry, and whoever believes in me will never be thirsty.'

GOD'S TABLE

We come from the beach where the surf is high
and the sun is bright in a cloudless sky.
We've hung our wetsuits out to dry
while we gather at God's table.

Eat the bread and drink the wine.
This feast of Christ is yours and mine,
inner Presence and outer sign
of Jesus at His table.

We've left the farm on a working day,
paddocks scattered with fresh cut hay.
It's time to meet with friends and pray
a thank you at God's table.

Eat the bread and drink the wine.
This feast of Christ is yours and mine,
inner Presence and outer sign
of Jesus at His table.

We come from a night of loss and pain,
of broken dreams and tears like rain,
to the One who heals again and again.
He's waiting at God's table.

Eat the bread and drink the wine.
This feast of Christ is yours and mine,
inner Presence and outer sign

of Jesus at His table.

We bring who we are to this sacred place,
richness of culture, richness of race,
and feel the warmth of God's embrace
when we gather at God's table.

Eat the bread and drink the wine.
This feast of Christ is yours and mine,
inner Presence and outer sign
of Jesus at His table.

Thought for the Day

The mystery of the Eucharist makes a oneness of our life in God and God's life in us.

48 Raising Lazarus

John 11: 32-46
...he cried with a loud voice, 'Lazarus, come out!' The dead man came out, his hands and feet bound with strips of cloth, and his face wrapped up in a cloth. Jesus said to them, 'Unbind him and let him go.'

COMING FORTH

Jesus, I don't know how many times
you've called me out of my tomb.
My life has been full of deaths,
some small, some not so little,
and before I knew it, I was wrapped
in a shroud and buried deep in a cave,
no strength to roll away the stone.
Each time, I thought, "This is it.
The sun will not rise tomorrow."
And hope died in the darkness.

Then always, you came by.

First, there was your voice,
the way you said my name
as though you've always known it,
and then, as the stone was moved,
there was the light that warmed my heart.
"Come forth!" you called. "Come forth!"
And I was up on my feet, and out of there,
as wobbly as a newborn child
but filled to the brim with life.

How do you do it, Lord?
How do you always know?

Your smile lights up the morning.
"I know all about tombs," you say.
"You forget, dear one,
that this is why I was born."

Thought for the Day

Love has a way of giving us new life when we are stuck in the darkness of a tomb.

49 Jesus at Simon's House

Matthew 26: 6-13
...a woman came to him with an alabaster jar of very costly ointment, and she poured it on his head as he sat at the table. But when the disciples saw it, they were angry and said, 'Why this waste?...'

THE ANOINTING OF JESUS

She was judged by the way she worshipped You.
It was not the done thing. She was over the top.
The righteous disciples condemned her
and criticised you, too, because
you accepted her gift with gratitude.

You said her name would be remembered
wherever your word was preached,
but was her name remembered?
Of course not. She was seen as interloper,
a woman of doubtful reputation
whose emotions ran out of control.

Today, I look at her and her love for you.
I look at you and the way you knew
what was in her beautiful heart.
Then I look at myself and wonder
about the judgements I place
on people who worship you
in much the same way as she did.

I can spend the whole day
reflecting on that.

Thought for the Day

Can we accept that other people love God as much as we do? That others rejoice in their religion as much as we rejoice in ours?

50 The Way, the Truth and the Life

John 14: 1-7
'…I will come again and will take you to myself, so that where I am, there you will be also….If you know me, you will know my Father also…'

BEAUTIFUL PRESENCE

Beautiful Presence, how can we name You?
Words are too small for the One who is all.
How can we speak of Your gentleness in us,
the warmth of our hearts in response to Your call?

Beautiful Presence, ocean of love,
strong as forever, soft as a dove,
words often fail us but this we know true,
You live within us as we live in You.

There have been times of spiritual blindness,
when error and pain have distorted our sight.
Beautiful Presence, You were there with us
to show us how darkness can turn into light.

Beautiful Presence, ocean of love,
strong as forever, soft as a dove,
words often fail us but this we know true,
You live within us as we live in You.

Nothing that happens to us will be wasted.
All of our living is grounded in grace.
Gently You take down the walls of division,
leading us on to a larger place.

Beautiful Presence, ocean of love,
strong as forever, soft as a dove,
words often fail us but this we know true,
You live within us as we live in You.

Thought for the Day

The closer God is to us, the more reluctant we are to name Him. We realise that God cannot be confined to ideas. Nonetheless, there is a deep knowledge of God in our hearts that goes far beyond words.

51 The True Vine

John 15: 1-17
'I am the true vine, and my Father is the vine grower. He removes every branch in me that bears no fruit. Every branch that bears fruit he prunes to make it bear more fruit...'

IN THE VINEYARD

This year will bring a good vintage.
We've had a cold winter, hot summer,
and fat bunches of dark pinot grapes
hang under the leaves, ready for picking.
No machines here. Not for this wine.
Each bunch, picked by hand, is laid
gently in the basket, a promise
of fine and exquisite taste.

Slowly, we move along the rows
under the hot Marlborough sun.
Wind combs the dry yellow grass
on the Wither hills, and a lone hawk
circles high above our heads.

In this part of the world
the grapes are picked in Lent,
a time when knowledge of the True Vine
is never far from the day's routine.
We are the branches, those ropes of wood
hanging between the eternal Vine
and the fruit ripe for harvest.
There is no separation.
The fruit from the eternal Vine,
gifted through its branches,

will go out to a thirsting world
bringing the fine and exquisite taste
of God.

What a feast!
What a celebration!

Thought for the Day

The True Vine is not separate from us. Whatever happens to the branches also happens to the Vine, and the deep nourishment of the Vine is also the nourishment of the branches.

52 The Ride into Jerusalem

Mark 11: 1-10
... Then those who went ahead and those who followed, were shouting, 'Hosanna! Blessed is the one who comes in the name of the Lord! Blessed is the coming kingdom of our ancestor David! Hosanna in the highest heaven!'

PALM SUNDAY

On the road to Wellington, he preached love
and the crowd went wild with enthusiasm.
They played guitars and sang songs about love,
waved pink heart-shaped balloons
and banners that said, Make Love not War.
The march got headlines in the papers.
TV cameras filmed it for the evening news.
This was the people's hero, everyone said,
a man who could change the world.
Some day he would be Prime Minister.

When they arrived in the city, he told them
what love was all about. Service, he said.
Selling that second car and giving the money
for a child who needed an operation.
Seeing all people as equal.
Judging no one. Visiting folk in prison.
Sharing food and shelter with those in need.
"If you have a spare room in your house,
why not invite a homeless person
to come and live with you?" he said.
"Love is not about words but action."

By the end of his speech,
most of the crowd had drifted away.
They called him a communist,
said he had a screw loose,
and they crucified him
with their anger.

Thought for the Day

We tend to see love as some kind of currency to be earned, to be carefully spent, to be given away with caution. That's not love. Love is reckless, extravagant. It comes without price and it has no need except to give itself away. Love is the outpouring of God in us and through us.

53 Jesus Washes the Disciples' Feet

John 13: 1-15

...Then he poured water into a basin and began to wash the disciples' feet and to wipe them with the towel that was tied around him...

GOD IN AN APRON

Jesus, it must have been difficult
for your disciples—those rough men
who stumbled along behind,
catching in you, glimpses of God
that made them half afraid.
They wouldn't know what to think
when their beloved Master, their Christ,
tucked a towel around his waist
and knelt humbly before them,
to wash their road-soiled feet.
It must have been a while
before any of them realised
that this beautiful service
contained one of the hardest lessons
they'd ever have to learn.

Jesus, it's still hard.
I can identify with the woman
who anointed your feet with her tears
but I need to dismantle all my ideas
about service, about worship, about religion,
before I can let you kneel before me
to demonstrate the extent of your love.

It is then that I catch a glimpse
of the power that created the universe.

Thought for the Day

In all of our religious thinking, do we dare to believe that God worships us?

54 The Last Supper

Matthew 26: 26-30
While they were eating, Jesus took a loaf of bread, and after blessing it, he broke it, gave it to his disciples, and said, 'Take, eat; this is my body.'…

THIS IS MY BODY

"Take and eat; this is my body."

Your body is broken as bread for us,
that in our brokenness we may understand
you are in all our crucifixions, big and small,
and you lead us always to resurrection.

"…this is my blood of the covenant,
which will be poured out for many
for the forgiveness of sins…"

Your disciples understood sacrifice.
It was a part of their traditional faith.
But this was bigger than simple atonement.
In your surrender to death you freed yourself
from the restrictions of one human life
to be available to all people.
Wherever blood is shed,
wherever there is pain,
wherever there is grief,
you are there closer than a breath
with the truth of life and death
and a greater life to come.

"… I shall not drink this fruit of the vine
until the day when I drink it with you
new in the kingdom of my Father."

You drink the new wine of the kingdom.
We drink the new wine of you
and through you, the kingdom
rests in us, a world without horizons,
a knowledge beyond words,
all of it contained in love.

And so singing, we go with you
to the Mount of Olives.

Thought for the Day

The deep mystery of the Eucharist defies words, although sometimes, poetry can take us near the edge of its meaning.

55 In the Garden of Gethsemane

Mark 14: 32-36

...he said to them, 'I am deeply grieved, even to death; remain here and keep awake.' And going a little farther, he threw himself on the ground and prayed that, if it were possible, the hour might pass from him...

FEAR AND LOVE

This was the time of bitter struggle.
Not the scourging, not the cross.
By then the inner agony was over
and you were ready for the tunnel of pain
that would lead to the open tomb.
It was here in this garden of sorrows
that you fought for the life you had worn
as lightly as a cloak, all these years.
You had talked of the tomorrow
but now that the time was near,
you wanted to hold on to incarnation:
the love of friends, the smell of wood-smoke,
the taste of fresh bread and wine,
warm days by the shore of the lake,
all of these were suddenly precious.

What if the decision had been reversed?
What if your story had been rewound
and played in a different way—
a life made comfortable with forgetting,
and a quiet sleep at the end? What then?

Where would we all be now?

Yours was the old struggle of gain and loss,
comfort and suffering, self and other,

but you took the thorns to heart
before they became your crown
and you said, "Your will be done."

So when it was time to walk
through that tunnel of pain,
you carried with you the larger gifts
of compassion and forgiveness
that have become ours.

Thought for the Day

We will all have our Gethsemane moments when we struggle with inner conflict, feeling ourselves to be utterly alone. We are not alone. When we see beyond the emotional storm, we realise that Jesus has been there all the time, praying with us.

56 Judas Iscariot

Matthew 26: 20-25

…'Truly I tell you, one of you will betray me.' And they became greatly distressed and began to say to him one after another, 'Surely not I, Lord?'…

THE BETRAYAL

Poor old Judas. He did a rotten thing
and we've never let him forget it.
Maybe he was afraid that Jesus
had strayed too far from orthodox teaching.
Maybe he was afraid that his master
would get them all killed.
Who knows what was in his mind?
All we know for certain, is that fear
is the great enemy of love.

So poor old Judas betrayed his Lord
with a kiss, the mark of friendship,
and then in bitter regret, followed him
out of this world, leaving behind
a legacy of hate from a Church
founded on love and forgiveness.

We all do it. Year after year, we project
our own fears and betrayals on Judas,
and in doing that, we fail to hear
the compassionate voice of Jesus
saying of Judas and of us,
"Father forgive them.
They know not what they do."

Thought for the Day

We all have our scapegoats, people like Judas Iscariot, Nero, Genghis Khan, Adolf Hitler, who sit in history like a row of coat pegs inviting us to hang up our blame. I see their evil because its potential resides also in me. That's something that Jesus understands with compassion.

57 The Trial

John 18: 33-40; 19:1
'For this I was born, and for this I came into the world, to testify to the truth…Pilate asked him, 'What is truth?'…he went out to the Jews again and told them, 'I find no case against him…'

CRUCIFY HIM!

An innocent man comes before judges
who have already decided on a verdict.
There is no one to defend this man.
One of his friends betrayed him,
one will deny him, and the others
are paralysed with fear.

He is taken to the governor,
while the people shout, "Crucify him!"
The women who are still with him
may not enter the Praetorium,
but above the cries of the crowd
they can hear the sound of the whip.

Crucify him! Crucify him!

When he comes out, crowned with thorns,
the shout becomes a roar, "Crucify him!"
and the crowd swarms like bees from a hive,
stinging him with every poisonous thought,
word and deed they've ever had.
Crucify him!

He bows his head.
He has taken upon himself
the history of the howling crowd,

evil posing as righteousness,
the powerful taking from the weak,
greed pretending to be democracy.
The eyes of this man hold
the crucifixions of the entire world.

I meet his gaze with a sorrowing heart.
When did I last notice his wounds
in my sisters and my brothers?
When did I object to media headlines
that shouted, "Crucify him! Crucify her!"
What action can I take now?

I look into his pain-filled eyes and ask,
Lord Jesus Christ, son of the living God,
tell me, what should I do?

Thought for the Day

I talk to God about my feelings of powerlessness when confronted with injustice.

58 Mary at the Cross

John 19: 25-27
Meanwhile, standing near the cross of Jesus were his mother, and his mother's sister, Mary the wife of Clopas, and Mary Magdalene...

HAIL MARY FULL OF GRACE

Mother of mothers,
your life was nailed to the cross with his,
and when his heart was pierced with a sword
the blade entered your heart as well,
for the pain of the child is also the mother's.
Holy Mary be with all women
who suffer the loss of their children.

Mother of Mysteries,
God appointed you before your birth
to be the bearer of Truth beyond human words,
and you, understanding the language of the heart,
gave a simple yes, to Truth's messenger.
Holy Mary, be with all those
who are afraid of both yes and no.

Mother of the Eucharist,
you gave up your body and blood
to bring the Christ into the world.
In you is pre-saged all the sacraments
and through you they came into being.
Holy Mary, may we stand with you
at the cross this Easter journey.

Thought for the Day

Every ending is also a beginning. I reflect on the beginnings and endings and new beginnings in my own life, and speak of them to Mary who journeyed that first Easter with her son.

59 The Crucifixion

John 23: 44-48

It was now about noon, and darkness came over the whole land until three in the afternoon, while the sun's light failed; and the curtain of the temple was torn in two. Then Jesus, crying with a loud voice, said, 'Father, into your hands I commend my spirit.' Having said this he breathed his last…

DOES IT HAVE TO BE?

My God, does it have to be crucifixion?
Death, yes. Sacrifice. But is it necessary
to have every detail of this man's service
scribbled out as in a child's drawing?
Nails through hands that healed the sick,
fed crowds and turned water into wine.
A spike crippling feet that walked
many miles in humility and obedience.
A sword piercing a heart that beat
in love for the world. And the thorns!
Why a crown of thorns for such a king?
Does every part of this beautiful life
need to be cancelled as though
it never existed? Why, God? Why?

Three days is too long to wait
for an answer.

Thought for the Day

The further we journey into the mystery of Easter, the more we know of the true meaning of love.

60 The Tomb

Matthew 27: 57-61
...So Joseph took the body and wrapped it in a clean linen cloth and laid it in his own new tomb, which he had hewn in the rock. He then rolled a great stone to the door of the tomb and went away…

WAITING FOR THE LIGHT

Lord, that burial cave in the rock
scarcely had time to get used to you,
before the stone was rolled away
and it was filled with the light
of your resurrection.

For me, it took much longer.
My little crucifixion had no room
for forgiveness and my darkness
was full of bitter thoughts
that I wrapped around myself as a shroud.

I did not see my small dying
as a letting go for something greater.
I was a victim. My hurt was my identity.
I thought that if I stayed in my tomb
I could remind friend and foe alike
of how badly I'd been treated.

The only problem with that is
there's no life, no light in a tomb.
So in the end, I took your hand
and let you lead me out,
on the way of forgiveness.

And it's true, it's really true!
Forgiveness rolls away the stone,
flooding the tomb with light.

Thought for the Day

It is time for spring-cleaning. Is there any corner or cupboard in my house where I have stored resentment, bitterness, negative judgements? How do these attitudes diminish my life?

61 The Resurrection

John 20: 11-18
... Jesus said to her, 'Mary!' She turned to him and said to him in Hebrew, 'Rabbouni!' (which means teacher)...Mary Magdalene went and announced to the disciples, 'I have seen the Lord'...

HE IS RISEN

He is risen! How can you doubt that, my friend?
See how the sun lifts the mist from the green hills?
Look at the multitude of trees with uplifted arms!
Listen to the massed choirs of bellbirds and tuis
pouring out their Hallelujahs!
Even the stream on its way to the sea
is singing a resurrection song.

Let me tell you something, my friend.
The death and resurrection story
is explanation, not transaction.
He is not some kind of insurance salesman,
dealing in life policies whose fulfilment
depends on our investment. Oh no!
That is much too small a view
of the abundant freedom offered
to us in those nail-marked hands.

It's about love, my friend. A cosmic love
that cannot be measured by the human mind
but can only be perceived, dimly, darkly, gratefully,
by the hungry human heart. Ultimately,
it's all there is. Just this endless love.

If you still have doubts, my friend,
stand outside the empty tomb
and listen to the way he says your name.

Thought for the Day

I will make time in this day to go into the garden of my heart and listen to him speaking to me as he speaks to no other.

62 The Road to Emmaus

Luke 24: 13-16, 28-31
...Then their eyes were opened and they recognised him; and he vanished from their sight. They said to each other, 'Were not our hearts burning within us while he was talking to us on the road, while he was opening the scriptures to us?'

MEETING JESUS ON THE ROAD

We saw him walking alone on the beach.
There was a nor'wester that swept across the sky
like a broom on the floor of a shearing shed,
and his coat was flapping behind him,
his hair wet with flying spray.
He laughed as he held his hands out to us,
and said, "Isn't this a beautiful morning?":
and we who'd been moaning about the weather,
suddenly saw the day bright with the energy of God
and we felt our hearts soar like gulls on the wind.
Later, we tried to describe it.
"Just like Emmaus," we said.

We were stuck in a motionless car.
There had been a rockfall in the gorge
and we'd been waiting for over an hour
for machines that worked in slow motion.
Rows of cars, pacing drivers, fretful kids—
it was some great start to the holiday!
Then she came along the road, in an apron,
carrying a cardboard box from car to car.
Sandwiches and muffins, she explained,
because we looked like we could be hungry.
No one knew where she'd come from

and, just as quietly, she disappeared,
leaving an oasis of peace behind her.
We felt the warmth in our hearts.
"Just like Emmaus," we said.

Then we knew that the road to Emmaus
lies not on a map of some ancient land,
but clean through the middle
of the hungry human heart.

Thought for the Day

Maybe I'll count the number of times I meet Jesus on the road of this coming day.

63 By the Sea of Tiberias

John 20: 15-17
...Peter felt hurt because he said to him the third time, 'Do you love me?' And he said to him, 'Lord, you know everything; you know that I love you.'

THE QUESTION

I thought this question had its place
on the shore of the Sea of Tiberias,
not in a carpark on Waterloo Quay.
You sit quietly in the passenger seat
watching a swoop of gulls behind
the incoming Cook Strait ferry,
and then you speak the question,
"Do you love me?"

"Yes," I answer. "Yes, Lord, I love you."

The wharf shudders against the weight
of the ship and the cargo doors crank open.
Covered trucks rumble across the ramp.
"Do you love me?" you ask again.

"Yes, Lord. I told you. I love you."

I feel that my answer is not enough for you.
More is needed and I don't know what to say.
The ferry disgorges long streams of traffic
into the bright afternoon. On each car,
a ball of sun bounces and splinters,
a welcome to the city of Wellington.
"Do you love me?" you repeat.

I am too close to tears for quick answer.
Your question is a blunt-edged shovel

digging deep and deeper yet
so that my first response is lost.
"Lord, you know everything about me.
You know that I love you."

The ferry is now empty and resting awhile
before the late afternoon sailing.
We sit in a gentle silence, you and I,
gazing out across the sun-washed harbour.
This is not Tiberias and I am not Peter,
and there is no instruction for the future,
just a daily question that shovels away
the less important layers of my life,
and an answer that comes
from the depths of my heart.

Thought for the Day

As a drop of water comes back to the ocean, so does my yearning for God find its way home to God's yearning for me. In that, I rest.

64 Come and See

John 1: 38-39
When Jesus turned and saw them following, he said to them, 'What are you looking for?' They said to him, 'Rabbi' (which translated means Teacher), 'where are you staying?' He said to them, 'Come and see.'...

HAERE MAI! TITIRO MAI!

He is at the railway station, newly off a train,
small backpack, red and black bush shirt, jeans,
a smile I've known since before I was born.
"Tena koe, e hoa," he says, and my heart dances.
He is with us! Actually here! Te tangatawhenua
speaking with the green voice of the land!
"Greetings, Friend," he says, and that smile
lights up the platform like a thousand suns.

"What are you doing here?" I ask,
already knowing that he is everywhere,
teaching in a village somewhere in India,
turning a prayer wheel in Tibet,
talking to children in Portugal,
healing in a street in Los Angeles.

There are other questions to ask him,
hundreds of words doing somersaults
out of this eager, dancing heart.
"How long will you be in this city?
Where are you staying, Lord?
What will you do while you are here?
Will you cure the deaf and the blind?
Will you give hope to hesitant lives?
Are you doing any workshops? Seminars?
Will you be interviewed on TV?"

By now, his smile has stopped other folk
who temporarily forget the road to work.
Their faces are open with the half-memory
of some purpose whispered to them
at the moment of their conception.
Like me, they don't know what that purpose is,
only that this man's smile holds the answer.

He lifts his hands to them, and to me.
"E hoa ma," he says. "Haere mai! Titiro mai!
Friends, come and see."

Thought for the Day

Whoever we are or wherever we are, this always is his invitation to us—come and see.

Postscript

This then, is the journey:
from the head to the heart;
from the city of learning
to the field wide open to the sun and rain;
from music dots on paper
to the sound of a Chopin nocturne;
from the structure of words
to the mystery beyond their meaning;
from the smallness of a manger
to the Love that holds the universe in being.

Glossary of Maori Words

Haere mai e Hehu	Come, Jesus
te whare iti	the small house
Aotearoa	New Zealand
Aoraki	the highest mountain in Aotearoa/New Zealand
e hoa	friend
e hoa ma	friends
tena koe	formal greeting to one person
te tanagatawhenua	the person of the land
Haere mai! Titiro mai!	Come! See!
tui	New Zealand bird
manuka	New Zealand tree
kawakawa	New Zealand tree with healing properties
kowhai	New Zealand tree